THE OFFICIAL ANNUAL 2023

Designed by **Daniel May**

A Grange Publication

© 2022. Published by Grange Communications Ltd., Edinburgh, under licence from The Liverpool Football Club. Printed in the EU.

Photographs © Liverpool FC and AG Ltd. & Getty Images

ISBN: 978-1-915295-50-7

CONTENTS

LFC HONOURS BOARD

ENGLISH LEAGUE CHAMPIONS
1900/01, 1905/06, 1921/22, 1922/23, 1946/47, 1963/64, 1965/66, 1972/73, 1975/76, 1976/77, 1978/79, 1979/80, 1981/82, 1982/83, 1983/84, 1985/86, 1987/88, 1989/90, 2019/20

FA CUP WINNERS
1965, 1974, 1986, 1989, 1992, 2001, 2006, 2022

LEAGUE CUP WINNERS
1981, 1982, 1983, 1984, 1995, 2001, 2003, 2012, 2022

EUROPEAN CUP/ CHAMPIONS LEAGUE WINNERS
1977, 1978, 1981, 1984, 2005, 2019

UEFA CUP WINNERS
1973, 1976, 2001

FIFA CLUB WORLD CUP WINNERS
2019

UEFA SUPER CUP WINNERS
1977, 2001, 2005, 2019

SECOND DIVISION CHAMPIONS
1893/94, 1895/96, 1904/05, 1961/62

FA YOUTH CUP WINNERS
1995/96, 2005/06, 2006/07, 2018/19

FOOTBALL LEAGUE SUPER CUP WINNERS
1985/86

CHARITY/COMMUNITY SHIELD WINNERS
1964*, 1965*, 1966, 1974, 1976, 1977*, 1979, 1980, 1982, 1986*, 1988, 1989, 1990*, 2001, 2006, 2022 (*shared)

FA WOMEN'S CHAMPIONSHIP WINNERS
2021/22

WOMEN'S SUPER LEAGUE CHAMPIONS
2013, 2014

RESERVE LEAGUE CHAMPIONS
1955/56, 1968/69, 1969/70, 1970/71, 1972/73, 1973/74, 1974/75, 1975/76, 1976/77, 1978/79, 1979/80, 1980/81, 1981/82, 1983/84, 1984/85, 1989/90, 1999/2000, 2007/08

LANCASHIRE LEAGUE CHAMPIONS
1892/93

TURNING THE TOWN RED

Over half a million people packed the city streets to hail the players and staff of Liverpool Football Club for all they achieved during an incredible 2021/22 season.

At the forefront of the victorious parade were the trophies won by both the men's and women's teams...while one bus proudly displayed the Carabao Cup and FA Cup, another showed off the FA Women's Championship title.

With renowned DJ and music producer Calvin Harris – the man responsible for unofficial club anthem One Kiss alongside Dua Lipa – playing a unique set for the duration of the parade, there were joyous scenes all along the 13.5km route that culminated in the city centre.

The turnout was simply amazing. Further proof, if ever needed, of just what a special club this is!

WE'RE SO GLAD JÜRGEN IS A RED...

"Delighted, humbled, blessed, privileged and excited."

These are the words Jürgen Klopp used to describe the news that his ongoing love affair with Liverpool Football Club will be extended until at least 2026.

It was in the midst of the thrilling finale to the 2021/22 season that Klopp put pen to paper on a new contract with the Reds and the announcement was music to the ears of Liverpudlians everywhere.

Since taking charge at Anfield in October 2015, the German has worked wonders; leading the team to glory on all fronts and making memories to last a lifetime.

He is without doubt one of the most popular managers in the club's history and the feelings are clearly mutual.

Klopp said: "There is just so much to love about this place. I knew that before I came here, I got to know it even better after I arrived and now I know it more than ever before.

"Like any healthy relationship, it always has to be a two-way street; you have to be right for each other. The feeling we were absolutely right for each other is what brought me here in the first place and it's why I've extended previously.

"This one is different because of the length of time we have been together. I had to ask myself the question: Is it right for Liverpool that I stay longer? Along with my two assistant managers, Pep Lijnders and Pete Krawietz, we came to the conclusion it was a 'Yes!'

"There is a freshness about us as a club still and this energises me. For as long as I have been here, our owners have been unbelievably committed and energetic about this club and it is clear that right now this applies to our future as much as I've ever known.

"In Billy Hogan and Julian Ward we have leaders throughout the club who are completely focused on renewal and refreshing so we can continue to compete at the very highest level.

In the early months of 2022, the first murmurs of a new song paying homage to Klopp were heard on coaches to away games and in pubs around the ground. Sung to the tune of the Beatles classic 'I Feel Fine', it quickly caught on and soon swept through stands. In case you've been living under a rock, it goes like this...

JÜRGEN SAID TO ME, YOU KNOW
WE'LL WIN THE PREMIER LEAGUE, YOU KNOW
HE SAID SO
I'M IN LOVE WITH HIM
AND I FEEL FINE
I'M SO GLAD, JÜRGEN IS A RED
I'M SO GLAD, HE DELIVERED WHAT HE SAID.

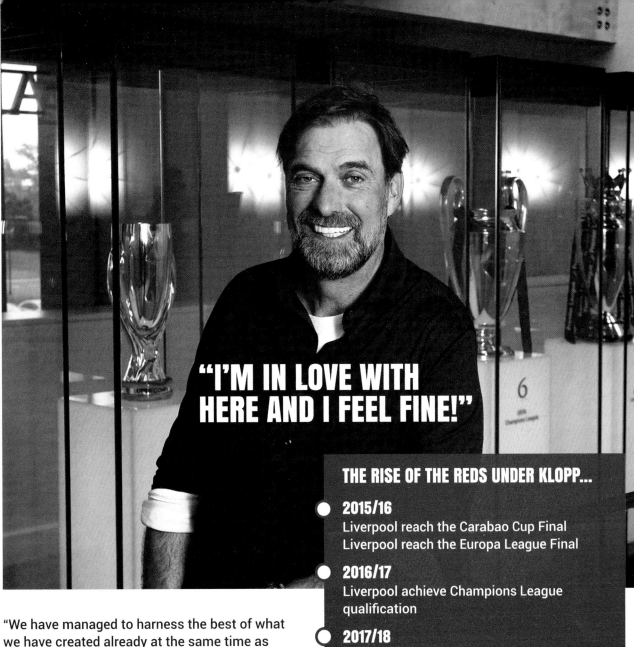

"I'M IN LOVE WITH HERE AND I FEEL FINE!"

THE RISE OF THE REDS UNDER KLOPP...

2015/16
Liverpool reach the Carabao Cup Final
Liverpool reach the Europa League Final

2016/17
Liverpool achieve Champions League qualification

2017/18
Liverpool reach the Champions League Final

2018/19
Liverpool win the Champions League
Liverpool finish Premier League runners-up

2019/20
Liverpool win the UEFA Super Cup
Liverpool win the FIFA World Club Cup
Liverpool win the Premier League

2020/21
Liverpool achieve Champions League qualification

2021/22
Liverpool win the Carabao Cup
Liverpool win the FA Cup
Liverpool finish Premier League runners-up
Liverpool reach the Champions League Final

2022/23
Liverpool win the FA Community Shield

"We have managed to harness the best of what we have created already at the same time as injecting fresh impetus into our environment. The new AXA Training Centre is a superb home for us and the fact that Anfield will grow even bigger soon with the Anfield Road development, I can't wait for that.

"We are a club that is constantly moving in the right direction. We have a clear idea of what we want; we have a clear idea of how we try to achieve it. That's always a great position to start from.

"When the owners brought the possibility to renew to me, I asked myself the question I've mused over publicly: do I have the energy and vibe to give of myself again what this amazing place requires from the person in the manager's office?

"I didn't need too long to answer in truth. The answer was very simple... I'm in love with here and I feel fine!"

Wembley Wizards - Part one

CARABAU CUP
WINNERS 2🏆22

3rd Round

 NORWICH CITY `0`

 LIVERPOOL `3`
Minamino (2), Origi

TEAM

Kelleher
Konaté
Gomez
Tsimikas (Robertson)
Bradley
Keïta (Morton)
Oxlade-Chamberlain
Jones (Henderson)
Minamino
Origi
Gordon

❯ The road to Wembley began with an all-Premier League tie at Carrow Road and, despite fielding a much-changed side, the Reds never looked in danger. Kaide Gordon, Conor Bradley and Tyler Morton all made their first-team debuts, while stand-in keeper Caoimhín Kelleher saved a penalty as goals from Taki Minamino (2) and Divock Origi completed a comfortable 3-0 victory.

4th round

	PRESTON NORTH END	0
	LIVERPOOL	2

Minamino, Origi

TEAM

Adrián
Gomez
Tsimikas
Matip (Phillips)
Williams
Oxlade-Chamberlain
(Dixon-Bonner)
Jones (Beck)
Morton
Minamino
Origi
Blair (Bradley)

> The Reds were made to work hard for this victory at Deepdale. Preston, of the Championship, spurned a number of gilt-edged opportunities to take the lead and it wasn't until the last half hour that Liverpool gained the upper hand. Taki Minamino once again broke the deadlock and a spectacular Divock Origi goal late in the game averted a potential upset.

Quarter-final

	LIVERPOOL 3	Liverpool won 5-4 on pens
	Oxlade-Chamberlain, Jota, Minamino	
	LEICESTER CITY 3	

TEAM

Kelleher
Gomez
Tsimikas (Beck)
Williams
Bradley (Jota)
Koumetio (Konaté)
Henderson (Keïta)
Oxlade-Chamberlain
Morton (Milner)
Firmino
Minamino

> Three days before Christmas the Anfield crowd was treated to a festive thriller that threatened to end Liverpool's cup aspirations. The Reds conceded three first-half goals and twice they had to fight back from a two-goal deficit. It needed a stoppage-time equaliser from Taki Minamino - his fourth goal of the competition — to force a penalty shoot-out in which Caoimhín Kelleher enhanced his growing reputation with two saves and Diogo Jota slotted home the winning kick.

Semi-final 1st leg

LIVERPOOL		0
ARSENAL		0

TEAM

Alisson

Alexander-Arnold (Williams)

Robertson

Van Dijk

Matip (Gomez)

Fabinho (Oxlade-Chamberlain)

Milner (Jones)

Henderson

Firmino

Minamino

Jota

> Liverpool failed to make home advantage pay as Arsenal produced a resolute defensive performance to keep the tie evenly balanced ahead of the return meeting in London. Not even the 24th minute dismissal of Granit Xhaka, for a reckless foul on Diogo Jota, could alter the course of the game and on a frustrating evening the Reds were restricted to very few genuine goalscoring opportunities.

Semi-final 2nd leg

ARSENAL		0
LIVERPOOL		2
Jota (2)		

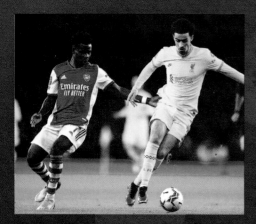

TEAM

Kelleher

Alexander-Arnold

Robertson

Van Dijk

Matip (Konaté)

Fabinho

Henderson (Milner)

Jones

Firmino (Williams)

Jota

Gordon (Minamino)

> With a place in the final up for grabs, Diogo Jota took centre-stage. The Portugal forward netted a memorable double, one in each half, to seal a Wembley date with Chelsea. His first came in the 19th minute, after a mazy run through the Gunners' defence. He then clinched victory 12 minutes from time with a deft finish in front of the travelling Liverpool supporters. Initially it was disallowed for offside but VAR proved that to be incorrect, sparking wild celebrations in the away end at the Emirates.

Final

 CHELSEA | **0**

 LIVERPOOL | **0**
Liverpool won
11-10 on penalties

LIVERPOOL'S TEAM

Kelleher
Alexander-Arnold
Matip (Konaté 90')
Van Dijk
Robertson
Henderson (Elliott 79')
Fabinho
Keïta (Milner 80')
Salah
Mané (Jota 80')
Díaz (Origi 97')

CHELSEA'S TEAM

Mendy (Arrizabalaga 120')
Chalobah
Thiago Silva
Rüdiger
Azpilicueta (James 57')
Kanté
Kovacic
Alonso
Mount (Lukaku 74')
Pulisic (Werner 74')
Havertz

> Liverpool's first Wembley final in six years culminated in penalty shoot-out glory and young Irish goalkeeper Caoimhín Kelleher was the unlikely hero.

In what was a pulsating encounter from start to finish, chances went begging at either end and both sides had goals ruled out for offside; Joël Matip for the Reds, Kai Havertz (twice) and Romelu Lukaku for Chelsea.

Not even extra-time could separate them and so it came down to the nerve-shredding lottery of penalties to decide the destiny of the season's first piece of silverware.

Remarkably, after ten kicks each, every outfield player had scored. Next it was the turn of the keepers and the tension was now almost unbearable. Kelleher stepped up first, kept his cool and duly converted, much to the relief of every Liverpudlian.

He then took his place back between the sticks as Kepa Arrizabalaga proceeded to blaze his effort high over the bar. It was 11-10 on pens and the League Cup was heading back to Anfield for a record-breaking 9th time.

HOW THE SHOOT-OUT UNFOLDED

MILNER	1	0	
	1	1	ALONSO
FABINHO	2	1	
	2	2	LUKAKU
VAN DIJK	3	2	
	3	3	HAVERTZ
ALEXANDER-ARNOLD	4	3	
	4	4	JAMES
SALAH	5	4	
	5	5	JORGINHO
JOTA	6	5	
	6	6	RÜDIGER
ORIGI	7	6	
	7	7	KANTÉ
ROBERTSON	8	7	
	8	8	WERNER
ELLIOTT	9	8	
	9	9	SILVA
KONATÉ	10	9	
	10	10	CHALOBAH
KELLEHER	11	10	
	11	10	KEPA MISSED!

"IT'S VERY SPECIAL TO WIN TROPHIES FOR THIS FOOTBALL CLUB, NO MATTER WHAT THE COMPETITION. IT WAS A GREAT OPPORTUNITY FOR US AND THANKFULLY WE'RE ON THE RIGHT SIDE OF IT. IT'S ALWAYS DIFFICULT WHEN IT GOES TO PENALTIES, IT'S NEVER NICE, BUT I THOUGHT THE LADS OVERALL DESERVED TO WIN."

Jordan Henderson

"I'M JUST DELIGHTED TO GET THE WIN AND IT'S A CLASS FEELING TO WIN IT AT WEMBLEY WITH ALL OF OUR FANS. IT'S SPECIAL. NEVER IN MY WILDEST DREAMS WOULD I HAVE THOUGHT I'D SCORE A PENALTY AT THE LIVERPOOL END, THE WINNING PENALTY. THAT'S JUST NEXT LEVEL. TO BE HONEST, I WAS GOING TO GO THE OTHER SIDE. AS I RAN UP, I JUST SAW OUT OF THE CORNER OF MY EYE THAT HE [KEPA] WAS DIVING THAT SIDE, SO I JUST WRAPPED MY FOOT AROUND IT. I DIDN'T MEAN IT TO GO THAT HIGH, TO BE HONEST."

Caoimhín Kelleher

"TO SEE US WIN WAS FANTASTIC. AND THE WAY IN WHICH IT CAME ABOUT, AFTER PENALTIES, YOU CAN SEE HOW MUCH THAT MEANT TO THE FANS. WE KNOW THEY ALWAYS SUPPORT US THROUGH THICK AND THIN, SO THEY CERTAINLY MADE THEMSELVES FELT ON THE PITCH THROUGHOUT THE GAME AND THE PENALTIES THEMSELVES. IT WAS FANTASTIC."

Luis Díaz

"KELLEHER IS THE BEST NUMBER TWO IN THE WORLD. HE HAD AN INCREDIBLE GAME. THE LIFE OF A NUMBER TWO IS YOU JUST HAVE TO BE READY WHEN YOU ARE CALLED AND THE GAME HE PLAYED TONIGHT WAS ABSOLUTELY INCREDIBLE. I CAN REMEMBER AT LEAST TWO INCREDIBLE SAVES, PROBABLY MORE, SO HE PROVES THAT THE DECISION TO LINE HIM UP WAS ABSOLUTELY RIGHT, AND THEN IN A VERY SPECTACULAR SHOOTOUT HE SHOWED THE WHOLE RANGE OF HIS SKILLSET."

Jürgen Klopp

ALISSON
BECKER

Position:
GOALKEEPER

Born:
NOVO HAMBURGO (BRAZIL)
2/10/1992

LFC debut:
V WEST HAM UNITED
12/8/2018

1st LFC goal:
V WEST BROMWICH ALBION
16/5/2021

FABINHO
TAVAREZ

Position:
MIDFIELDER

Born:
CAMPINAS (BRAZIL)
23/10/1993

LFC debut:
V PARIS SAINT-GERMAIN
18/9/2018

1st LFC goal:
V NEWCASTLE UNITED
26/12/2018

FA CUP
WINNERS 2022

3rd Round

LIVERPOOL	**4**
Gordon, Fabinho (2), Firmino	
SHREWSBURY TOWN	**1**

TEAM

Kelleher
Bradley
Robertson (Tsimikas)
Van Dijk
Konaté
Fabinho
Jones
Dixon-Bonner (Firmino)
Morton (Norris)
Gordon (Frauendorf)
Woltman (Minamino)

 An under-strength Liverpool recovered well from the shock of falling behind to their League One opponents and eventually went on to record a routine-looking victory. 17-year-old Kaide Gordon got the comeback underway with his first senior goal but it wasn't until late in the second half, following the introduction of substitute Roberto Firmino, that a place in round four was assured.

4th round

LIVERPOOL Jota, Minamino, Elliott	**3**
CARDIFF CITY	**1**

TEAM

Kelleher
Alexander-Arnold
Tsimikas (Robertson)
Van Dijk
Konaté
Keïta (Elliott)
Henderson (Thiago)
Jones (Díaz)
Firmino
Minamino (Milner)
Jota

> Despite languishing near the wrong end of the Championship table, Cardiff frustrated Liverpool for long periods of this game and it wasn't until the second half that it turned in favour of the hosts. Three goals in a 23-minute spell eventually saw the Reds fully exert their authority on this game. Among the highlights were a first glimpse of new signing Luis Díaz and a stunning goal from Harvey Elliott on his return from a serious injury.

5th round

LIVERPOOL Minamino (2)	**2**
NORWICH CITY	**1**

TEAM

Alisson
Tsimikas
Milner
Gomez
Konaté
Henderson (Morton)
Oxlade-Chamberlain
Jones (Elliott)
Minamino
Jota (Díaz)
Origi (Mané)

> Two first-half strikes by Taki Minamino put Liverpool on course for a fourth victory of the season over Norwich and, although they failed to add to that tally, their place in the last eight never seemed under threat, even when the visitors pulled a goal back. It was the first time since taking charge at Anfield that Klopp had taken his team beyond the fifth round of this competition.

Quarter-final

| | NOTTINGHAM FOREST | 0 |
| | LIVERPOOL | 1 |

Jota

TEAM

Alisson
Tsimikas
Gomez
Van Dijk
Konaté
Fabinho (Thiago)
Keïta (Henderson)
Oxlade-Chamberlain (Díaz)
Firmino
Jota
Elliott (Minamino)

> The quarter-final saw a long-lost rivalry, forged back in the late 1970s, renewed at the City Ground. It had been over two decades since the sides last met and the eagerly anticipated occasion lived up to expectations as a tight, tense, affair ensued. Forest, chasing promotion back to the Premier League, had already taken a number of big scalps in previous rounds and Liverpool did well to avoid joining that list thanks to a solitary Diogo Jota goal 12 minutes from time.

Semi-final

| | MANCHESTER CITY | 2 |
| | LIVERPOOL | 3 |

Konaté, Mané (2)

TEAM

Alisson
Alexander-Arnold
Robertson
Van Dijk
Konaté
Fabinho
Thiago (Jones)
Keïta (Henderson)
Mané (Jota)
Salah
Díaz (Firmino)

> Liverpool burst out of the starting blocks at a sun-baked Wembley and tore into City from the first whistle. Ibrahima Konaté headed in the opener after just nine minutes and Sadio Mané quickly doubled the advantage by capitalising on a moment of hesitancy by the opposition keeper. A one-sided half ended with Mané netting again, this time with a spectacular right-footed volley, on the stroke of half-time to give the Reds a seemingly unassailable lead. City hit back after the break to reduce the deficit and scored again in injury time but it wasn't enough.

Final

Wembley Stadium
Saturday 14 May 2022
Attendance: 84,897

 CHELSEA `0`

 LIVERPOOL `0`

Liverpool won 6-5 on penalties

LIVERPOOL'S TEAM

Alisson
Alexander-Arnold
Robertson (Tsimikas 111)
Van Dijk (Matip 90)
Konaté
Keïta (Milner 74)
Henderson
Thiago
Salah (Jota 33)
Mané
Díaz (Firmino 98)

CHELSEA'S TEAM

Mendy
Chalobah (Azpilicueta 105)
Thiago Silva
Rüdiger
James
Jorginho
Kovacic (Kanté 66)
Alonso
Mount
Pulisic (Loftus-Cheek 105, Barkley 119)
Lukaku (Ziyech 85)

> For the second time in three months, an epic battle between Liverpool and Chelsea culminated in penalty shoot-out drama beneath the Wembley arch as the Reds completed a memorable domestic cup double by capturing the FA Cup for an eighth time in the club's history.

In what was their first appearance in this showpiece fixture for ten years, Liverpool had to overcome the double blow of losing both Mohamed Salah and Virgil van Dijk through injury but were clearly the better team on the day.

Only the post denied Luis Díaz and Andy Robertson from winning the game in normal play and just like in the Carabao Cup final, spot-kicks were required to eventually separate the two sides.

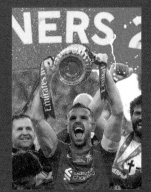

Sadio Mané looked set to be the hero when he stepped up to take the Reds' fifth penalty, but Chelsea were handed a lifeline when his effort was saved. That is, until Alisson denied Mason Mount, leaving Kostas Tsimikas to step up and become the unlikely cup-winning hero.

HOW THE SHOOT-OUT UNFOLDED

	0	1	ALONSO
MILNER	1	1	
	1	1	AZPILICUETA MISSED
THIAGO	2	1	
	2	2	JAMES
FIRMINO	3	2	
	3	3	BARKLEY
ALEXANDER-ARNOLD	4	3	
	4	4	JORGINHO
MANÉ MISSED	4	4	
	4	5	ZIYECH
JOTA	5	5	
	5	5	MOUNT MISSED
TSIMIKAS	6	5	

"WE'RE HERE TO LIFT TROPHIES, WE WORK SO HARD ALL SEASON. TO COME HERE AND GET OVER THE LINE MEANS A LOT TO EVERYONE. THE FANS DESERVE IT, THE WHOLE CLUB. IT'S A BIG MOMENT FOR US, WE HAVEN'T BEEN IN THIS FINAL FOR SOME TIME SO TO WIN IT WAS SPECIAL."

Jordan Henderson

"IT'S VERY, VERY SPECIAL FOR ME. THE MANAGER ASKED ME WHICH NUMBER I WANT. I SAY NUMBER SEVEN. HE ASKS ME WHY SO FAR? I SAY I WANT NUMBER SEVEN. AND NUMBER SEVEN GAVE ME THE OPPORTUNITY TO WIN THE GAME. I CHOOSE THE RIGHT SIDE AND I SCORE. AND I AM VERY HAPPY WITH THAT. I AM NOT THE GREEK SCOUSER, I AM THE SCOUSE GREEK!"

Kostas Tsimikas

"IT'S AMAZING, WE DID SUCH A GOOD PERFORMANCE. IT WAS A SHAME WE DIDN'T SCORE. IT WAS A PROPER FIGHT, WE KEPT A CLEAN SHEET, AND THEN AFTERWARDS THE BOYS WERE UNBELIEVABLE SCORING THE GOALS. I JUST HAD TO SAVE THE LAST ONE."

Alisson

"I COULDN'T BE MORE PROUD OF MY BOYS; THE SHIFT THEY PUT IN, HOW HARD THEY FOUGHT, EARLY CHANGES. ALL OF THESE THINGS, MISSING GOOD CHANCES, OVERCOMING GOOD MOMENTS FROM CHELSEA, THEN HAVING REALLY GOOD MOMENTS OURSELVES. IT WAS AN INCREDIBLE GAME, A NERVE-WRACKING SHOOT-OUT, MY NAILS ARE GONE. WE ARE MENTALITY MONSTERS. IN THE END THERE MUST BE ONE WINNER AND THAT WAS US TODAY."

Jürgen Klopp

VIRGIL
VAN DIJK

Position:
DEFENDER

Born:
BREDA (HOLLAND)
8/7/1991

LFC debut:
V EVERTON
5/1/2018

1st LFC goal:
V EVERTON
5/1/2018

IBRAHIMA
KONATÉ

Position:
DEFENDER

Born:
PARIS (FRANCE)
25/5/1999

LFC debut:
V CRYSTAL PALACE
18/9/2021

1st LFC goal:
V BENFICA
5/4/2022

5

GOING UP ⬆

Liverpool FC Women are back where they belong and on the rise once again.

Matt Beard's side enjoyed a highly successful 2021/22 campaign, in which they secured their return to the Women's Super League and clinched the Championship title.

An unforgettable season began with a 1-0 defeat at home to London City but from that moment on the team went from strength to strength.

They lost just once more in the league, on the final day when there was nothing at stake.

Those losses bookended an impressive 20-game unbeaten run that saw the Reds eventually complete their dual target of promotion and the title.

A mid-season run of seven straight wins propelled them into pole position and with two games still to play they wrapped up the formalities with a 4-2 victory away to Bristol City.

They topped the table by 11 points and a record crowd turned out at Prenton Park to see them presented with the trophy — an occasion they marked in style by hammering Sheffield United 6-1.

To cap a memorable season, the victorious Liverpool FC Women's squad and staff then paraded the silverware to the fans at Anfield during the half-time interval of the first team's Premier League game against Tottenham.

FA WOMEN'S CHAMPIONSHIP MILESTONES 2021/22

Biggest home win: **6-1 v Sheffield United, 24 April 2022**
Biggest away win: **6-0 v Blackburn Rovers, 9 January 2022**
Longest winning run: **7 matches**
Longest unbeaten run: **20 matches**

"I'M INCREDIBLY PROUD OF THE PLAYERS AND THE STAFF WITH WHAT WE'VE ACHIEVED. WE WORK INCREDIBLY HARD AT THE TRAINING GROUND, ON THE TRAINING PITCH AND WE'VE GOT THE REWARDS FOR THAT. IF YOU WORK HARD AND YOU'VE GOT A GOOD ATMOSPHERE AND YOU'VE GOT RESPECT AMONGST EACH OTHER, THEN THESE ARE THE THINGS THAT YOU CAN ACHIEVE."

Matt Beard (manager)

"IT'S JUST FANTASTIC TO HAVE THE PRIVILEGE AND HONOUR OF BEING CAPTAIN AND ALSO TO WIN A LEAGUE TITLE - THAT'S UNBELIEVABLE STUFF REALLY. YOU CAN'T DREAM OF THESE THINGS AND I'M JUST SO HAPPY THAT WE HAVE MANAGED TO DO IT TOGETHER AS A SQUAD AND WITH THIS GROUP OF PLAYERS AND STAFF THAT WE HAVE. IT'S ALSO SPECIAL FOR OUR FANS AS WELL, GIVING THEM SMILES ON THEIR FACES AGAIN. IT'S UNBELIEVABLE."

Niamh Fahey (captain)

"IT'S JUST A FANTASTIC FEELING. IT'S ONE THAT WE HAVE WORKED HARD FOR ALL SEASON AND I'M JUST BUZZING THAT WE ARE BACK UP IN THE TOP LEAGUE. WE'VE BEEN RUTHLESS, WE'VE BEEN RESILIENT AND WE'VE BEEN EVERYTHING WE WANTED TO BE FROM THE START OF THE SEASON. I'M PROUD OF EVERY SINGLE ONE OF THE GIRLS IN THE SQUAD, I'M PROUD OF EVERY MEMBER OF THE STAFF AND WE REALLY DESERVE IT THIS SEASON."

Rachel Furness

"THE TOGETHERNESS HAS BEEN KEY, NOT JUST ON THE PITCH BUT OFF IT AS WELL. IT'S A COLLECTIVE EFFORT, SOMETHING I'VE NEVER EXPERIENCED BEFORE. IT'S NOT JUST US [THE TEAM]; THE STAFF PREPARE US WEEK IN, WEEK OUT, MAKE SURE WE ARE READY AND IT REALLY IS A COLLECTIVE."

Rachael Laws

"IT'S AN AMAZING FEELING. IT HAS BEEN A LONG TIME FOR US TO WAIT AND WE ARE JUST BUZZING TO GO BACK UP - AND WE DESERVE TO GO BACK UP. CREDIT TO EVERYONE, WE DEFEND FROM THE FRONT. LAWSY HAS BEEN ABSOLUTELY CLASS FOR US AGAIN THIS SEASON, WE'VE KEPT A LOT OF CLEAN SHEETS, OUR FOOTBALL HAS BEEN REALLY GOOD. WE HAVE STEPPED UP EVERY TIME THIS SEASON AND SHOWN WHAT WE ARE ABOUT; THE ENVIRONMENT, THE GROUP WE'VE GOT, THE TOGETHERNESS IS UNREAL."

Rhiannon Roberts

"I'VE BEEN WEARING THE LIVERPOOL SHIRT SINCE I WAS BORN. I'M 21 NOW AND JUST WON MY FIRST TITLE WITH THEM. HOPEFULLY THERE'S MANY MORE. TITLES DON'T HAPPEN OVERNIGHT, THEY ARE A LOT OF HARD WORK WEEK IN, WEEK OUT AND THIS WIN PROVES THAT."

Missy Bo Kearns

AWARDS

FA Women's Championship Player of the Season: **Rachael Laws**
FA Women's Championship Manager of the Year: **Matt Beard**
FA Women's Championship Golden Glove: **Rachael Laws**
Liverpool FC Women's Standard Chartered Player of the Season: **Leanne Kiernan**
Liverpool FC Women's Players' Player of the Season: **Rachael Laws**
Liverpool FC Women's Young Player of the Season: **Taylor Hinds**
Liverpool FC Women's Club Person of the Season: **Niamh Fahey**

HOW THE FA WOMEN'S CHAMPIONSHIP WAS WON

London City (h)	0-1
Watford (a)	3-2
Bristol City (h)	0-0
Crystal Palace (h)	2-1
Coventry United (a)	2-0
Sheffield United (a)	2-0
Lewes (h)	2-0
Blackburn Rovers (h)	0-0
Durham (a)	2-0
Sunderland (a)	3-1
Blackburn Rovers (a)	6-0
Watford (h)	1-0
Crystal Palace (a)	4-0
Coventry United (h)	3-0
Sunderland (h)	3-0
London City (a)	1-1
Charlton Athletic (a)	1-0
Charlton Athletic (h)	0-0
Durham (h)	3-0
Bristol City (a)	4-2
Sheffield United (h)	6-1
Lewes (a)	1-2

FA WOMEN'S CHAMPIONSHIP LEAGUE TABLE 2021/22

		P	W	D	L	GF	GA	GD	PTS
1	Liverpool	22	16	4	2	49	11	+38	52
2	London City Lionesses	22	13	2	7	35	22	+13	41
3	Bristol City	22	11	4	7	43	28	+15	37
4	Crystal Palace	22	11	4	7	35	39	-4	37
5	Charlton Athletic	22	10	4	8	27	18	+9	34
6	Durham	22	10	4	8	30	28	+2	34
7	Sheffield United	22	9	6	7	34	31	+3	33
8	Lewes	22	9	2	11	23	24	-1	29
9	Sunderland	22	6	6	10	23	32	-9	24
10	Blackburn Rovers	22	5	2	15	17	41	-24	17
11	Coventry United	22	5	7	10	18	32	-14	12
12	Watford	22	2	5	15	18	46	-28	11

APPEARANCES (LEAGUE ONLY)

Taylor Hinds	22*	Jade Bailey	14
Leanne Kiernan	22*	Ashley Hodson	13
Ceri Holland	21	Carla Humphrey	12
Melissa Lawley	21	Katie Stengel	12
Niamh Fahey	20	Megan Campbell	11
Rachel Furness	19	Meikayla Moore	9
Missy Bo Kearns	19	Georgia Walters	5
Rachael Laws	19	Rianna Dean	3
Jasmine Matthews	19	Rylee Foster	2
Yana Daniëls	18	Hannah Silcock	2
Charlotte Wardlaw	18	Charlotte Clarke	1
Rhiannon Roberts	17	Lucy Parry	1
Leighanne Robe	15		

*ever-presents

GOALSCORERS (LEAGUE ONLY)

Leanne Kiernan	13	Taylor Hinds	3
Katie Stengel	8	Rianna Dean	2
Yana Daniëls	4	Ashley Hodson	2
Missy Bo Kearns	4	Melissa Lawley	2
Niamh Fahey	3	Rhiannon Roberts	2
Rachel Furness	3	Charlotte Wardlaw	1

WORDSEARCH
LIVERPOOL'S LEAGUE OF NATIONS

The Reds' first team squad is an eclectic mix, comprising of players born all over the world. Below is a list of the countries represented in the Anfield dressing room, but can you find them on this grid by searching horizontally, vertically and diagonally?

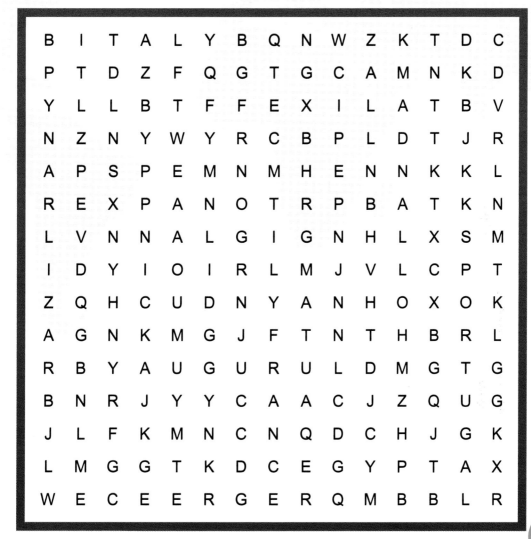

```
B  I  T  A  L  Y  B  Q  N  W  Z  K  T  D  C
P  T  D  Z  F  Q  G  T  G  C  A  M  N  K  D
Y  L  L  B  T  F  F  E  X  I  L  A  T  B  V
N  Z  N  Y  W  Y  R  C  B  P  L  D  T  J  R
A  P  S  P  E  M  N  M  H  E  N  N  K  K  L
R  E  X  P  A  N  O  T  R  P  B  A  T  K  N
L  V  N  N  A  L  G  I  G  N  H  L  X  S  M
I  D  Y  I  O  I  R  L  M  J  V  L  C  P  T
Z  Q  H  C  U  D  N  Y  A  N  H  O  X  O  K
A  G  N  K  M  G  J  F  T  N  T  H  B  R  L
R  B  Y  A  U  G  U  R  U  L  D  M  G  T  G
B  N  R  J  Y  Y  C  A  A  C  J  Z  Q  U  G
J  L  F  K  M  N  C  N  Q  D  C  H  J  G  K
L  M  G  G  T  K  D  C  E  G  Y  P  T  A  X
W  E  C  E  E  R  G  E  R  Q  M  B  B  L  R
```

ANSWERS ARE ON PAGE 61

(Bonus points awarded if you can also list the name of at least one player next to their country of origin!)

◯ BRAZIL ◯ GERMANY ◯ ITALY

◯ COLOMBIA ◯ GREECE ◯ PORTUGAL

◯ EGYPT ◯ GUINEA ◯ SCOTLAND

◯ ENGLAND ◯ HOLLAND ◯ SPAIN

◯ FRANCE ◯ IRELAND ◯ URUGUAY

THIAGO
ALCÂNTARA

Position:
MIDFIELDER

Born:
SAN PIETRO VERNOTICO (ITALY)
11/4/1991

LFC debut:
V CHELSEA
20/9/2020

1st LFC goal:
V SOUTHAMPTON
8/5/2021

6

JAMES
MILNER

Position:
MIDFIELDER

Born:
LEEDS (ENGLAND)
4/1/1986

LFC debut:
V STOKE CITY
9/8/2015

1st LFC goal:
V ASTON VILLA
26/9/2015

7

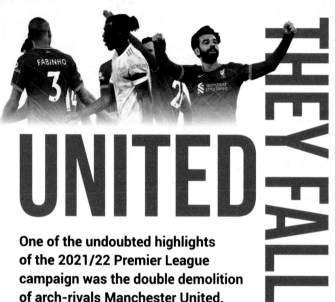

UNITED THEY FALL

One of the undoubted highlights of the 2021/22 Premier League campaign was the double demolition of arch-rivals Manchester United.

For just the sixth time in three decades, Liverpool defeated United home and away but that tells only half the story of a glaringly obvious and unparalleled gulf in class between these old enemies.

At Old Trafford in October the visitors raced into a four-goal lead by half-time; Naby Keïta, Diogo Jota and Mo Salah, with a brace, silencing the home fans. The Egyptian then completed his hat-trick to seal a famous 5-0 victory, Liverpool's best ever at this particular venue.

When the teams met again, at Anfield in April, any hopes of revenge that United harboured were quickly extinguished. Liverpool's first-half display was widely lauded as one of the finest of recent times and their 2-0 advantage at the break didn't do it justice.

Come the final whistle, a further two goals ensured the end result was a much fairer reflection of the home side's superiority and the travelling supporters sneaked out thankful in the knowledge that their side had got off lightly.

The margin of victory in both games could and should have been more but no one of a Liverpool persuasion was complaining.

Where this fixture is concerned we had ventured into unprecedented territory and 9-0 over two games was certainly something to savour.

9 - 0
OVER TWO GAMES WAS CERTAINLY SOMETHING TO SAVOUR

PRIDE OF THE MERSEY

Liverpool emphatically regained local bragging rights in 2021/22 and reaffirmed their overall dominance in the long-running story of the Merseyside derby.

Comprehensive home and away victories for the Reds – their 96th and 97th in the fixture, compared to 67 for Everton – left Evertonians feeling as blue as the colour of their team's shirts.

At Goodison on the first night of December, with former Liverpool boss Rafael Benítez in the Everton manager's chair, Jürgen Klopp's team turned on the style to leave their hosts wallowing in misery.

After goals from Jordan Henderson and Mo Salah had put the visitors 2-0 ahead inside 20 minutes, it looked like the record books were about to be rewritten - until they allowed Everton a glimmer of hope.

Thankfully, Demarai Gray's goal proved to be nothing more than a consolation and normal service was soon resumed with Salah netting another after half-time, before Diogo Jota completed a 4-1 rout.

The return meeting at Anfield in April was a bit closer and it wasn't until the second-half that Liverpool took full control, but the destiny of the three points were never in real doubt.

It was just after the hour mark when Andy Robertson popped up at the far post to head in the opener and five minutes from time, 'supersub' Divock Origi pounced to torment Everton for the sixth and final time when he sealed another memorable victory in front of the Kop.

The city once again reverberated to the Liverpool sound as the red half celebrated the completion of another league double.

LUIS DÍAZ

The first-ever Colombian to play for Liverpool, Luis Díaz became an instant hit at Anfield following his move from Porto during the January transfer window in 2022. One of the most exciting attackers to emerge from South America in recent years, Díaz quickly established himself as a firm favourite of the fans and was an instrumental figure in the team that won the Carabao and FA Cup, as well as challenging strongly for both the Premier and Champions Leagues during his first season on Merseyside.

What did you know about Liverpool before joining?

"It's a club that I've followed for a good while now, and I've always watched them play. It's no secret that the Premier League is one of the best leagues around and I've followed the football here and watched it since I was a boy. And as for Liverpool, I don't think I need to say much about them that hasn't been said. It's a great club, a real reference in the game, which has won many cups and league titles, and so Liverpool has always been my choice."

Are you surprised at how quickly you've been able to adapt to your new surroundings?

"I wanted to settle as quickly as possible and to get to know the style of play and feel comfortable. In training and on the field, I think I've managed to develop a good understanding with my teammates – and I think that's been down to both them and the coaching staff, who have helped me in this settling-in period. They have been a great help to me [and] I want to just keep doing my best. From a personal point of view, it's just how I dreamed of starting."

Has training and playing alongside your new teammates been as you expected?

"I'm really, really happy to be sharing a training ground and the pitch with them. I had admired them from afar but when you are up close and training with them, you can tell a lot more than

LIFE BEFORE LIVERPOOL

2016 to 2017

Barranquilla FC
Apps: 42   Goals: 3

2017 to 2019

Atletico Junior
Apps: 108   Goals: 20

Honours won:
Copa Colombia (2017),
Categoria Primera A (2018, 2019),
Superliga Colombiana (2019)

2019 to 2022

FC Porto
Apps: 125   Goals: 41

Honours won:
Primeira Liga (2020, 2022),
Taca de Portugal (2020, 2022),
Supertaca Candido de Oliveira (2020)

if you're watching on TV. It's just not the same watching on TV or from the stands. You appreciate it [more] when you're alongside them. And it's not just up front but all over the park that quality amongst every player. They've all got huge skill, ability in football terms, and also tactically as well – they're very aware and have great appreciation of the game tactically."

And how have you found working under a manager like Jürgen Klopp?

"Incredible! That's a single word you can use for him from the short time we've spent working together. He's a very humble, down-to-earth person, very calm. He tries to ensure all his players are happy, and for me that's very important. At the start, I think it was more about him telling me what I've been doing up to now. He was trying to put across to me that all it was about was for me to keep doing what I've been used to. He wanted me to know that I'd been performing very well up to now and that I should just try to keep on doing more of the same: to play my football with joy and happiness, while obviously incorporating the preferred tactical plans and instructions into my game."

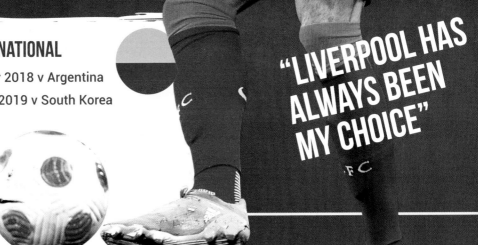

COLOMBIAN INTERNATIONAL

Debut: 11 September 2018 v Argentina

First goal: 26 March 2019 v South Korea

Apps: 35*   **Goals:** 8*

Honours won:
Joint Golden Boot winner alongside Lionel Messi at the 2021 Copa America with four goals

correct up to the start of the 2022/23 season

"LIVERPOOL HAS ALWAYS BEEN MY CHOICE"

N A B Y
KEÏTA

Position:
MIDFIELDER

Born:
CONAKRY (GUINEA)
10/2/1995

LFC debut:
V WEST HAM UNITED
12/8/2018

1st LFC goal:
V SOUTHAMPTON
5/4/2019

36

ROBERTO
FIRMINO

Position:
FORWARD

Born:
MACEIÓ (BRAZIL)
2/10/1991

LFC debut:
V STOKE CITY
9/8/2015

1st LFC goal:
V MANCHESTER CITY
21/11/2015

EURO
REVIEW 2021/22

Despite cruising through the group phase with a one hundred per cent record – the first British club to do so – and then impressively overcoming each hurdle the knockout rounds had to offer, Liverpool's dream of Champions League glory ultimately fizzled out on a frustrating night in Paris.

AC Milan, Porto, Atlético Madrid, Internazionale, Benfica and Villarreal had all been beaten en route to an eagerly anticipated showdown with Real Madrid in the final at the Stade de France.

The two teams had met in the final of this competition twice before: in 2018, the Spaniards had triumphed 3-1 in Kiev to claim the trophy but back in 1981 it was the Reds who emerged victorious, running out 1-0 winners in the city that was now playing host to the 2022 finalists.

It was the first time in the competition's history that the same two teams had met in the final three times - but unfortunately for Liverpool it was a case of third time unlucky.

Despite enjoying long periods of possession and going close with a Sadio Mané shot that hit the post, it was Real Madrid who broke the deadlock through Vinicius Junior, against the run of play, in the 59th minute.

There was no further scoring, and Liverpool's bid to be crowned Kings of Europe for a seventh time, in what was their 10th final appearance, ended in disappointment.

LIVERPOOL'S ROAD TO PARIS

GROUP B

MILAN (H)	3-2	
PORTO (A)	5-1	
ATLÉTICO MADRID (A)	3-2	
ATLÉTICO MADRID (H)	2-0	
PORTO (H)	2-0	
MILAN (A)	2-1	

		PLD	PTS
1.	LIVERPOOL	6	18
2	ATLÉTICO MADRID	6	7
3	PORTO	6	5
4	MILAN	6	4

ROUND OF 16

1st leg

 INTERNAZIONALE | 0 - 2 | LIVERPOOL

2nd leg

 LIVERPOOL | 0 - 1 | INTERNAZIONALE

Agg: 2-1

QUARTER-FINAL

1st leg

 BENFICA | 1 - 3 | LIVERPOOL

2nd leg

 LIVERPOOL | 3 - 3 | BENFICA

Agg: 6-4

SEMI-FINAL

1st leg

 LIVERPOOL | 2 - 0 | VILLARREAL

2nd leg

 VILLARREAL | 2 - 3 | LIVERPOOL

Agg: 5-2

FINAL Saturday 28 May 2022 • Attendance: 75,000 • Referee: Clément Turpin (France)

 LIVERPOOL | 0

 REAL MADRID | 1

LIVERPOOL'S TEAM

- Alisson
- Alexander-Arnold
- Robertson
- Van Dijk
- Konaté
- Fabinho
- Thiago (Firmino 77)
- Henderson (Keïta 77)
- Salah
- Mané
- Díaz (Jota 65)

REAL MADRID'S TEAM

- Courtouis
- Carvajal
- Mendy
- Militão
- Alaba
- Modrić (Ceballos 90)
- Casemiro
- Kroos
- Valverde (Camavinga 86)
- Benzema
- Vinicius (Rodrygo 90+3)

DOUBLE DELIGHT FOR
MIGHTY MO

Mo Salah created history in 2022 when he became the first Liverpool player to win the country's two major player of the year awards for the second time in his Anfield career...

Mo Salah! Mo Salah! Mo Salah! Running down the wing. Salah la-la-la la-ahh, The Egyptian king!

The Reds' Egyptian King scooped both the Professional Footballers' Association and the Football Writers' Association accolades to repeat a feat he first achieved in 2018.

It was a just reward for a campaign in which he was, for a spell, simply unstoppable in front of goal, netting 31 times in all competitions.

The previous Liverpool players to be awarded both prizes in the same season are Terry McDermott, Kenny Dalglish, John Barnes and Luis Suárez, but in doing it for a second time Salah has now raised the bar even higher.

OTHER PERSONAL ACCOLADES THAT CAME MO'S WAY DURING THE 2021/22 SEASON...

→ Premier League Golden Boot

→ Premier League Playmaker of the Season

→ PFA Fans' Player of the Year

→ Premier League Player of the Month (October)

→ Premier League Goal of the Month (October v Manchester City)

→ Liverpool's Standard Chartered Men's Player of the Season

IT WAS ALSO A CAMPAIGN IN WHICH HE...

→ Became Liverpool's all-time record goalscorer in the European Cup/ Champions League

→ Moved into the Reds' top ten all-time leading goalscorers list

→ Surpassed Didier Drogba as the top scoring African player in Premier League history

→ Reached 100 goals in the Premier League quicker (in 151 games) than any other Liverpool player

→ Scored over 20 Premier League goals for a club-record fourth time

LIVERPOOL'S PREVIOUS PLAYER OF THE YEAR RECIPIENTS

PROFESSIONAL FOOTBALLER'S ASSOCIATION AWARD

1980	Terry McDermott	2006	Steven Gerrard
1983	Kenny Dalglish	2014	Luis Suárez
1984	Ian Rush	2018	Mo Salah
1988	John Barnes	2019	Virgil van Dijk

2022 — MO SALAH

FOOTBALL WRITERS' ASSOCIATION AWARD

1974	Ian Callaghan	1988	John Barnes
1976	Kevin Keegan	1989	Steve Nicol
1977	Emlyn Hughes	1990	John Barnes
1979	Kenny Dalglish	2009	Steven Gerrard
1980	Terry McDermott	2014	Luis Suárez
1983	Kenny Dalglish	2018	Mo Salah
1984	Ian Rush	2020	Jordan Henderson

2022 — MO SALAH

NEW CONTRACT

In July 2022, Liverpool supporters everywhere received the news they had been longing to hear: their hero Mo Salah had committed his long-term future to the club. Taking a break from his summer holiday in Greece, the Kop's 30-year-old Egyptian King announced that he'd put pen to paper on a new deal that extends his stay at Anfield way beyond the five years he's already completed.

MOHAMED
SALAH

11

Position:
FORWARD

Born:
BASYOUN (EGYPT)
15/6/1992

LFC debut:
V WATFORD
12/8/2017

1st LFC goal:
V WATFORD
12/8/2017

JORDAN
HENDERSON

C

Position:
MIDFIELDER

Born:
SUNDERLAND (ENGLAND)
17/6/1990

LFC debut:
V SUNDERLAND
13/8/2011

1st LFC goal:
V BOLTON WANDERERS
27/8/2011

WELCOME TO LIVERPOOL:

DARWIN NÚÑEZ

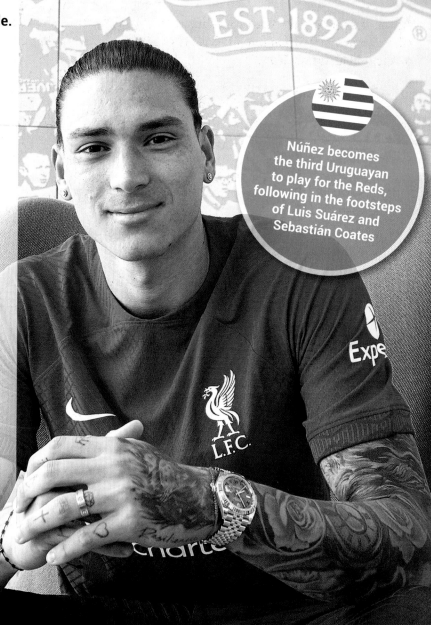

From Montevideo to Merseyside. Find out more about our big summer signing of 2022...

- He was born on 24 June 1999 in Artigas, Uruguay

- His first professional club was Peñarol, for whom he made 22 competitive appearances

- He then moved to UD Almería in Spain, scoring 16 goals in 32 games

- He scored against Peru on his international debut in October 2019

- In 2020 he joined Benfica and was the top scorer in Portugal last season

- Two of his 34 goals that season came in the Champions League quarter-final at Anfield

- In June 2022 he was unveiled as a Reds' player

- His squad number at Liverpool is 27, the shirt previously worn by Divock Origi

Núñez becomes the third Uruguayan to play for the Reds, following in the footsteps of Luis Suárez and Sebastián Coates

DARWIN NÚÑEZ IN HIS OWN WORDS...

ON SIGNING FOR LIVERPOOL...
"As a kid you dream of going far and I dreamt of being able to play in Europe, but I didn't expect to get as far as a great club like Liverpool. It's a pleasure to be here in Liverpool."

FIRST IMPRESSIONS OF THE CLUB...
"When I arrived at the training ground, I was really surprised to see the set-up and the structure and all the trophies here. It's a massive club."

PLAYING AT ANFIELD FOR BENFICA...
"It was a spectacular experience seeing what the fans are like in the stadium. It's an incredible atmosphere."

SCORING GOALS...
"As a striker you live off the goals that you score but I find that when one goes in, more follow."

TEAMWORK...
"The main thing for me is to help the team because they're going to need me and I'm going to need them."

COMPETITION FOR PLACES...
"There'll be a lot of competition between the forwards here but it will be healthy competition. We're all here to help each other out so everything goes well for everybody."

WHAT HE HOPES TO ACHIEVE...
"I came to Liverpool to win trophies; I want to win a lot."

THE IMMEDIATE FUTURE...
"I want to make sure that I keep performing well, keep on the right path and don't deviate from that path, while always remaining humble and keeping my feet on the ground."

DEALING WITH ANY PRESSURE...
"I don't feel pressured by anything or anybody. I think the only pressure on a player comes from within to ensure things go well."

PLAYING FOR JÜRGEN KLOPP...
"It's great for any player that a manager can improve and polish you as a player, and I think that Klopp is going to help me hugely. It will be great that Klopp can show me lots more things. I'm still only 22 and I've got lots that I can still learn."

LEARNING ENGLISH (AND SCOUSE!)...
"My English is very bad. I've got to make sure I learn it quickly, without a doubt. I think it's really important that a player can speak English because it helps you a lot in everything. But I have got one phrase, 'Boss tha!'"

Jürgen Klopp on Núñez...
"DARWIN IS A WONDERFUL PLAYER; ALREADY REALLY GOOD BUT SO MUCH POTENTIAL TO GET EVEN BETTER. THAT'S WHY IT'S SO EXCITING, TO BE HONEST. HIS AGE, HIS DESIRE, HIS HUNGER TO BE EVEN BETTER THAN HE CURRENTLY IS."

MEET THE OTHER NEW BOYS...

FÁBIO CARVALHO

BORN: **LISBON, 30 AUGUST 2002**
PREVIOUS CLUB: **FULHAM**
POSITION: **FORWARD**
SQUAD NUMBER: **28**

CARVALHO

A Portugal under-21 international, who also represented England at youth level, he came through the ranks at Fulham and was part of the squad that won promotion to the Premier League last season.

"IT'S JUST AN AMAZING FEELING TO BE HERE AT ONE OF THE BIGGEST CLUBS IN THE WORLD, IF NOT THE BIGGEST. SO I'M JUST HAPPY TO BE HERE. ONCE YOU HEAR THAT LIVERPOOL ARE INTERESTED, THERE'S ONLY ONE THOUGHT IN YOUR MIND, WHICH IS TO JOIN THEM AND TRY TO BE IN AND AROUND THE TEAM. HOPEFULLY I CAN ACHIEVE BIG THINGS."

Fábio Carvalho

CALVIN RAMSAY

BORN: **ABERDEEN, 31 JULY 2003**
PREVIOUS CLUB: **ABERDEEN**
POSITION: **RIGHT-BACK**
SQUAD NUMBER: **22**

A player with his hometown club since the age of nine, he's a Scotland under-21 international and last season won the Scottish Football Writers' Young Player of the Year award.

RAMSAY

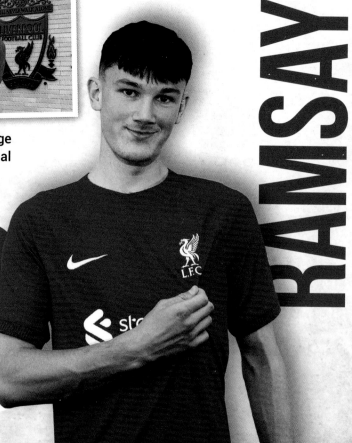

"THERE WAS A LOT OF SPECULATION. BUT AS SOON AS I HEARD THE SPECULATION FROM LIVERPOOL, I JUST WANTED TO GET IT DONE, I KNEW THAT'S THE CLUB THAT I WANTED TO GO TO. I'LL TRY TO DO MY BEST AND I'M LOOKING FORWARD TO IT. THE MAIN THING IS JUST TO GET ON THAT PITCH AT ANFIELD AND TRY TO PUT MY MARKER DOWN."

Calvin Ramsay

DIOGO
JOTA

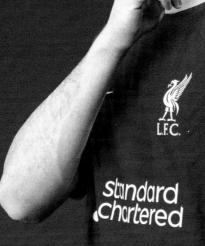

Position:
FORWARD

Born:
PORTO (PORTUGAL)
4/12/1996

LFC debut:
V LINCOLN CITY
24/9/2020

1st LFC goal:
V ARSENAL
28/9/2020

LUIS DÍAZ

Position:
FORWARD

Born:
BARRANCAS (COLOMBIA)
13/1/1997

LFC debut:
V CARDIFF CITY
6/2/2022

1st LFC goal:
V NORWICH CITY
19/2/2022

23

ANDY
ROBERTSON

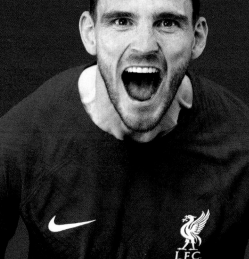

Position:
DEFENDER

Born:
GLASGOW (SCOTLAND)
11/3/1994

LFC debut:
V CRYSTAL PALACE
19/8/2017

1st LFC goal:
V BRIGHTON & HOVE ALBION
13/5/2018

26

KOP QUIZ

WHO AM I?

Can you guess the Liverpool player from their former clubs?

1. BARCELONA, BAYERN MUNICH...

_____

2. LEEDS UNITED, NEWCASTLE UNITED, ASTON VILLA, MANCHESTER CITY...

_____

3. PEÑAROL, ALMERÍA, BENFICA...

_____

4. AL MOKAWLOON, BASEL, CHELSEA, AS ROMA...

_____

5. GRONINGEN, CELTIC, SOUTHAMPTON...

_____

6. BARRANQUILLA, ATLÉTICO JUNIOR, PORTO...

_____

GOLDEN AGE

Can you place the following Liverpool players in the correct order, going from youngest to oldest?

JOËL MATIP	1	
HARVEY ELLIOTT	2	
DARWIN NÚÑEZ	3	
JAMES MILNER	4	
ANDY ROBERTSON	5	
MO SALAH	6	

TRUE OR FALSE?

1. JORDAN HENDERSON was born in Liverpool – T / F

2. ROBERTO FIRMINO is the only Liverpool player to have scored in a World Club Cup Final – T / F

3. JAMES MILNER won the Premier League with Manchester City – T / F

4. LUIS DÍAZ and DARWIN NÚÑEZ were teammates before joining Liverpool – T / F

5. KOSTAS TSIMIKAS is the first Greek-born Liverpool player – T / F

6. CURTIS JONES scored his first Liverpool goal against Everton in the FA Cup – T / F

ANSWERS ARE ON PAGE 61

■□■■ ODD ONE OUT Circle the *incorrect* answer for each of the following...

1 TEAMS LIVERPOOL HAVE PLAYED IN THE FA CUP FINAL...

Arsenal   Everton   Chelsea   Manchester United   Manchester City   Newcastle United

2 CITIES IN WHICH LIVERPOOL HAVE BEEN CROWNED CHAMPIONS OF EUROPE...

Paris   London   Rome   Munich   Madrid   Istanbul

3 COLOURS LIVERPOOL HAVE WORN AS AN AWAY STRIP...

Yellow   White   Brown   Green   Orange   Purple

4 TROPHIES LIFTED BY JORDAN HENDERSON AS LIVERPOOL CAPTAIN...

Premier League   FA Cup   Europa League   Champions League   Super Cup   League Cup

5 PLAYERS WHO MADE THEIR DEBUT FOR LIVERPOOL IN 2021/22...

Kaide Gordon   Tyler Morton   Luis Díaz   Ibrahima Konaté   Conor Bradley   Diogo Jota

6 MANAGERS WHO HAVE WON EUROPEAN TROPHIES FOR LIVERPOOL...

Bob Paisley   Kenny Dalglish   Rafael Benítez   Jürgen Klopp   Bill Shankly   Joe Fagan

(365 DAYS) NAME THE YEAR

Use the clues to work out what year the following events took place...

1 Liverpool win the European Cup for the first time – Kenny Dalglish is signed from Celtic – Emlyn Hughes is named Player of the Year

2 Steven Gerrard plays his last game for the Reds – Jürgen Klopp becomes Liverpool manager – Divock Origi scores his first and only hat-trick for the club

3 Liverpool reach the final of the European Cup Winners' Cup – Roger Hunt is the club's top scorer – the Reds beat Everton to lift the Charity Shield at Goodison

4 Trent Alexander-Arnold is born – Liverpool have joint managers – Michael Owen scores but is then sent off at Old Trafford

5 The first all-Merseyside cup final takes place – Ian Rush wins the Golden Boot – Alan Kennedy is a penalty shoot-out hero in Rome

6 Liverpool play three times at the Millennium Stadium in Cardiff – Robbie Fowler is sold to Leeds United – the UEFA Cup Final is decided by a 'Golden' own goal

51

THE 'CANNONBALL' KID

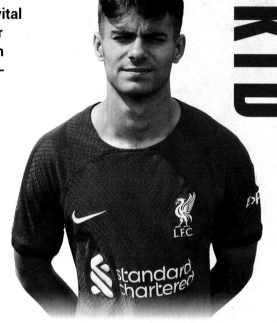

He was the quick-thinking ball boy who played a vital role in the famous Champions League victory over Barcelona in 2019. Three years later and he's been firing in goals at a prolific rate for Liverpool under-18s…let's meet Academy starlet OAKLEY CANNONIER.

→ Born in Leeds on 6 May 2004

→ Joined Liverpool aged 11

→ Was one day short of his 15th birthday on the night of the Barcelona game

→ During the 2021/22 season he scored 41 goals in all competitions

→ In August 2022 he signed a new long-term deal with the club

THAT NIGHT V BARCA…

"Liverpool were obviously getting beat, so the assistant manager told our coach that the ball needs to be in rapid for the intensity of the game. Everything had to be quick. It still is a bit mad. People getting in touch on social media calling me a Liverpool legend. It does make me feel proud, it is a massive moment. But I want to be a footballer, not a ball boy."

LEAVING HOME AT SUCH AN EARLY AGE…

"I could've gone to a few different clubs, but I just always wanted to play for Liverpool. It was a no-brainer. I went to house parents in Year 7 so I could go to school in Liverpool, it was easier than travelling from Leeds every single day. I tried giving myself the best chance to be prepared."

GOALSCORING HEROES…

"When I was younger, I used to love Torres. But then after he went to Chelsea, it was Suárez. I loved those two. They were just goalscorers and they were always the decisive players and I wanted to be like that."

TRAINING WITH THE FIRST-TEAM & MEETING JÜRGEN…

"It was a really good experience. The boss came up to me and he was like, 'I just need to thank you' for what I did. The players are all really welcoming and they're so good…just Thiago getting the ball and doing things I've not really seen before, I thought, 'Wow'."

HIS STYLE OF PLAY…

"I used to assist more, a number ten. Dropping deep has helped me. But with the goals I have scored, I've also found myself in good situations. I don't like not scoring, to be honest. It's not selfish but I put pressure on myself to score. I just want to be the best I can. I've scored a few goals and I'm just looking to kick on from where I am now."

DARWIN
NÚÑEZ

Position:
FORWARD

Born:
ARTIGAS (URUGUAY)
24/6/1999

LFC debut:
V MANCHESTER CITY
30/07/2022

1st LFC goal:
V MANCHESTER CITY
30/07/2022

27

JOËL
MATIP

Position:
DEFENDER

Born:
BOCHUM (GERMANY)
8/8/1991

LFC debut:
V BURTON ALBION
23/8/2016

1st LFC goal:
V CRYSTAL PALACE
26/10/2016

32

TRENT
ALEXANDER-ARNOLD

Position:
DEFENDER

Born:
LIVERPOOL (ENGLAND)
7/10/1998

LFC debut:
V TOTTENHAM HOTSPUR
25/10/2016

1st LFC goal:
V TSG 1899 HOFFENHEIM
15/8/2017

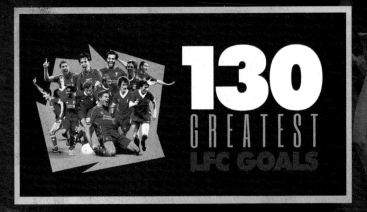

130 GREATEST LFC GOALS

Over the course of Liverpool's long and illustrious history, they have scored more than ten thousand goals. In June 2022, to commemorate the club's 130th anniversary, a countdown of the goals deemed to be the greatest since the dawn of televised football in 1964 began – be it in terms of importance, iconic status or simply sheer quality – and it culminated with supporters voting these as the top 10...

To watch every goal in the countdown visit - ▶ www.youtube.com/c/LiverpoolFC

1 | DIVOCK ORIGI V BARCELONA
Champions League Semi-Final 2nd leg, 7 May 2019

The second of two he scored on this night but the one for which he will forever be remembered. From a 'corner taken quickly', he applied the finishing touch to complete one of the most remarkable comebacks in history.

2 | STEVEN GERRARD V WEST HAM UNITED
FA Cup Final, 13 May 2006

It was the 90th minute and Liverpool trailed 3-2 when the captain shrugged off the effects of cramp to unleash an unstoppable volley from 30 yards out that arrowed into the net like a missile and revived hopes of more cup glory.

3 | STEVEN GERRARD V AC MILAN
Champions League Final, 25 May 2005

A powerful glancing header from the edge of the box; at the time it seemed nothing more than a mere consolation, but it was a goal that proved to be the catalyst for the miracle of Istanbul and Liverpool's fifth European Cup success.

4 | TERRY MCDERMOTT V TOTTENHAM HOTSPUR
First Division, 2 September 1978

On an afternoon when it rained goals at Anfield, this far-post header, following a move that saw the ball travel from one end of the pitch to the other in just a matter of seconds, was the icing on the cake of a famous 7-0 win.

5 | KENNY DALGLISH V CLUB BRUGGE
European Cup Final, 10 May 1978

With a delicate dink over the keeper, the new King of the Kop crowned his first season at the club by scoring the goal that retained the European Cup for Liverpool on a memorable night at Wembley.

6 | DAVID FAIRCLOUGH V SAINT-ETIENNE
European Cup Quarter-Final 2nd leg, 16 March 1977

Just six minutes remained, and Liverpool were heading out of the competition, until 'Supersub' kept his cool in front of a baying Kop to slot home the goal that kept them on course to conquer Europe for the first time.

7 | KENNY DALGLISH V CHELSEA
First Division, 3 May 1986

In the final league game of his first season as player/manager, the Reds' number seven controlled the ball on his chest just inside the box before hitting the back of the net with an unerring finish at Stamford Bridge to clinch the title.

8 | IAN RUSH V EVERTON
FA Cup Final, 10 May 1986

Having scored earlier in the game to draw Liverpool level, the club's master marksman finished off a flowing move with typical pinpoint accuracy to complete a famous 3-1 victory that secured the coveted League and FA Cup double.

9 | ALAN KENNEDY V REAL MADRID
European Cup Final, 27 May 1981

Nine minutes from time, on a tense night in Paris, Liverpool's number three was the unlikely hero as he barged through the Spanish defence to break the deadlock with an angled drive to ensure the Reds were Kings of Europe for a third time.

10 | IAN ST JOHN V LEEDS UNITED
FA Cup Final, 1 May 1965

An acrobatic header at Wembley that ended a 73-year long wait for a first-ever FA Cup, the game was deep into extra-time and heading for a replay when the Saint somehow twisted his body in mid-air to nod home the winner.

VICTORY SHIELD

MANCHESTER CITY		1	3		LIVERPOOL

Alexander-Arnold, Salah, Núñez

Liverpool claimed the first silverware of the 2022/23 season courtesy of a thrilling victory over Manchester City at the King Power Stadium in Leicester.

The annual curtain-raiser to the campaign – that pits the Premier League champions against the FA Cup winners – was claimed by the Reds following a 3-1 win, with Trent Alexander-Arnold, Mo Salah and Darwin Núñez scoring the goals.

It completed a treble of domestic trophy triumphs in the calendar year of 2022, was the club's first success in the Community Shield since 2006 and the 16th time they had lifted the shield in total.

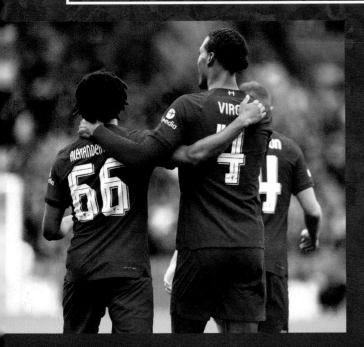

THE FA COMMUNITY SHIELD 2022

CELEBRATING ENGLAND FOOTBALL

2022/23 FIXTURE TRACKER

*All fixtures subject to change

L.F.C.

 PREMIER LEAGUE

2022

August

6	Fulham	(A)	☐ ☐
15	Crystal Palace	(H)	☐ ☐
22	Manchester United	(A)	☐ ☐
27	Bournemouth	(H)	☐ ☐
31	Newcastle United	(H)	☐ ☐

September

3	Everton	(A)	☐ ☐
10	Wolverhampton Wanderers	(H)	☐ ☐
18	Chelsea	(A)	☐ ☐

October

1	Brighton & Hove Albion	(H)	☐ ☐
8	Arsenal	(A)	☐ ☐
15	Manchester City	(H)	☐ ☐
19	West Ham United	(H)	☐ ☐
22	Nottingham Forest	(A)	☐ ☐
29	Leeds United	(H)	☐ ☐

November

| 5 | Tottenham Hotspur | (A) | ☐ ☐ |
| 12 | Southampton | (H) | ☐ ☐ |

December

| 26 | Aston Villa | (A) | ☐ ☐ |
| 31 | Leicester City | (H) | ☐ ☐ |

2023

January

2	Brentford	(A)	☐ ☐
14	Brighton & Hove Albion	(A)	☐ ☐
21	Chelsea	(H)	☐ ☐

February

4	Wolverhampton Wanderers	(A)	☐ ☐
11	Everton	(H)	☐ ☐
18	Newcastle United	(A)	☐ ☐
25	Crystal Palace	(A)	☐ ☐

March

4	Manchester United	(H)	☐ ☐
11	Bournemouth	(A)	☐ ☐
18	Fulham	(H)	☐ ☐

April

1	Manchester City	(A)	☐ ☐
8	Arsenal	(H)	☐ ☐
15	Leeds United	(A)	☐ ☐
22	Nottingham Forest	(H)	☐ ☐
25	West Ham United	(A)	☐ ☐
29	Tottenham Hotspur	(H)	☐ ☐

May

6	Brentford	(H)	☐ ☐
13	Leicester City	(A)	☐ ☐
20	Aston Villa	(H)	☐ ☐
28	Southampton	(A)	☐ ☐

 FA CUP

January 7	3rd round	V		H/A	☐ ☐
January 28	4th round	V		H/A	☐ ☐
March 1	5th round	V		H/A	☐ ☐
March 18	Quarter-final	V		H/A	☐ ☐
April 22	Semi-final	V		N	☐ ☐
June 3	FINAL	V		N	☐ ☐

 **LEAGUE CUP**

November 8/9	3rd round	V		H/A	☐ ☐
December 20/21	4th round	V		H/A	☐ ☐
January 10/11	5th round	V		H/A	☐ ☐
January 25	Semi-final 1st leg	V		H/A	☐ ☐
February 1	Semi-final 2nd leg	V		H/A	☐ ☐
February 26	FINAL	V		N	☐ ☐

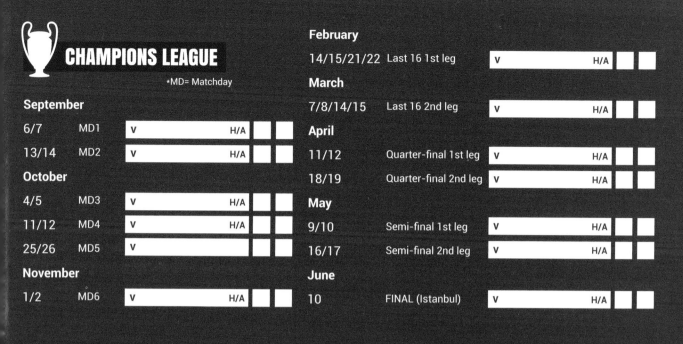

CHAMPIONS LEAGUE

*MD= Matchday

September				
6/7	MD1	V	H/A	
13/14	MD2	V	H/A	

October				
4/5	MD3	V	H/A	
11/12	MD4	V	H/A	
25/26	MD5	V		

November				
1/2	MD6	V	H/A	

February				
14/15/21/22	Last 16 1st leg	V	H/A	

March				
7/8/14/15	Last 16 2nd leg	V	H/A	

April				
11/12	Quarter-final 1st leg	V	H/A	
18/19	Quarter-final 2nd leg	V	H/A	

May				
9/10	Semi-final 1st leg	V	H/A	
16/17	Semi-final 2nd leg	V	H/A	

June				
10	FINAL (Istanbul)	V	H/A	

THE QUIZ ANSWERS!

PAGE 29 - WORDSEARCH

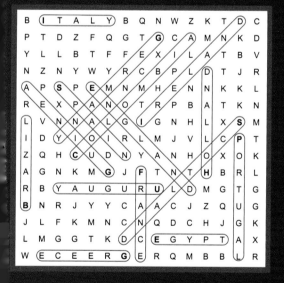

COUNTRY OF ORIGIN

BRAZIL — Alisson, Fabinho, Roberto Firmino
COLOMBIA — Luis Díaz
EGYPT — Mo Salah
ENGLAND — Trent Alexander-Arnold, Joe Gomez, James Milner, Jordan Henderson, Alex Oxlade-Chamberlain, Curtis Jones, Harvey Elliott
FRANCE — Ibrahima Konaté
GERMANY — Joël Matip
GREECE — Kostas Tsimikas
GUINEA — Naby Keïta
HOLLAND — Virgil van Dijk
IRELAND — Caoimhín Kelleher
ITALY — Thiago Alcântara
PORTUGAL — Diogo Jota, Fabio Carvalho
SCOTLAND — Andy Robertson, Calvin Ramsay
SPAIN — Adrián
URUGUAY — Darwin Núñez

You're Boss! Well done.

PAGE 40 - KOP QUIZ

WHO AM I?
1. Thiago Alcântara
2. James Milner
3. Darwin Núñez
4. Mo Salah
5. Virgil Van Dijk
6. Luis Díaz

GOLDEN AGE
1. James Milner
2. Joël Matip
3. Mo Salah
4. Andy Robertson
5. Darwin Núñez
6. Harvey Elliott

TRUE OR FALSE?
1. False
2. True
3. True
4. False
5. False
6. True

ODD ONE OUT
1. Manchester City
2. Munich
3. Brown
4. Europa League
5. Diogo Jota
6. Kenny Dalglish

NAME THE YEAR
1. 1977
2. 2015
3. 1966
4. 1998
5. 1984
6. 2001

YOU'LL NEVER